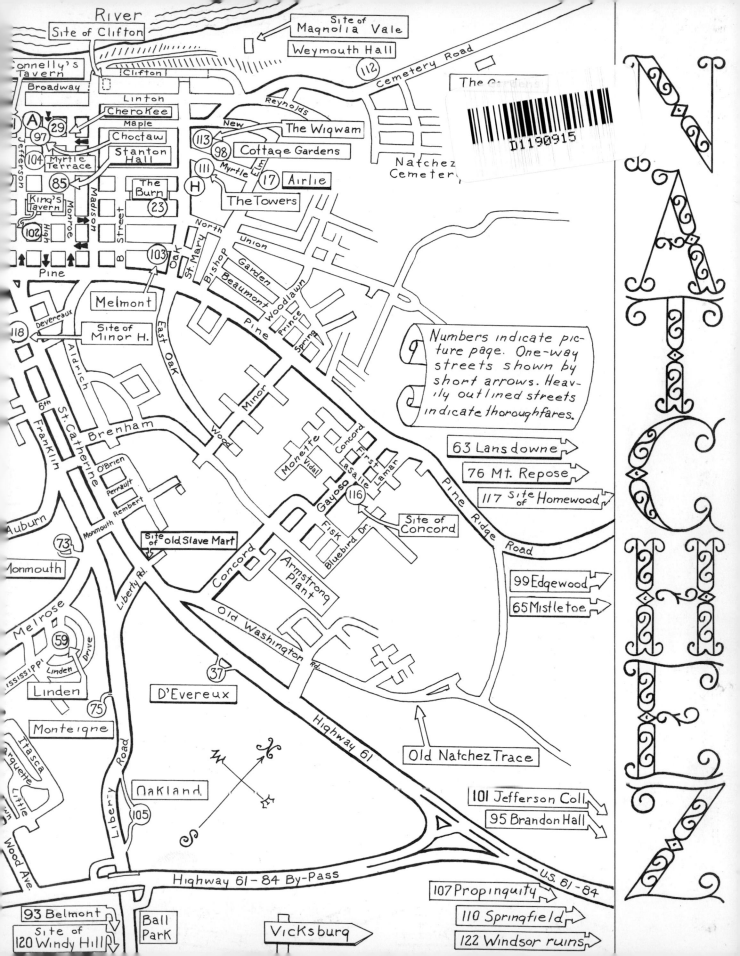

NATCHEZ

Museum City of the Old South

Death lurked among the shadows along the old Natchez Trace

NATCHEZ

Museum City of the Old South

By ROBERT GORDON PISHEL

Revised Edition

MAGNOLIA PUBLISHING COMPANY
TULSA, OKLAHOMA

Library of Congress Catalog Card No: 58-14368

Guide Book edition published March, 1955

Lithographed by Commercial Publishers,
Tulsa, Oklahoma
Printed in the United States of America

Dedication

*It is to the City of Natchez, Mississippi, to its people, and
to its pilgrims that this book is dedicated, for enshrined here
in this veritable museum, as nowhere else, is the architecture,
the memories, and the romance of the Old South of long ago.*

Contents

Mecca on the Mississippi

NATCHEZ! Once it was only an Indian word, but now it is a magic word that each year draws thousands upon thousands of people from all over the world to one of our little cities in the Southland. What is its magic? Why do these visitors make such a pilgrimage and then vow that they will return some day? Let me tell you.

Natchez is the romantic Old South of song and story so complete and so compact and so compelling that few who hear its siren call can resist its lure. Here like a cross-section in a museum is laid bare the entire history of a Southern locality from the day of the American Indian to the day of the present American. Although other cities in the South present similar historical offerings, very few, if any, except Natchez come close to the atmosphere and feeling of those times of long ago when cotton was *really* King and the hooped-skirt was worn *every* day.

Make no mistake about it. Natchez is the deep South all right. This is not a motion picture set—it is authentic. This is the land of magnolias and azaleas, of cotton and Negroes, of bourbon and branch water, and hooped-skirts and honeyed words. This is Spanish moss and Confederate flags and riverboat legends and red ravines and hush puppies and beaten biscuits. But most of all, Natchez is the old houses with the tall, graceful columns bright with fresh paint shining whitely beneath the green live oaks. To make it even more authentic, many of the homes contain not only the original furnishings but also descendants of the original owners who lived here over a century ago.

The only earlier Americans to dwell upon these high Mississippi River bluffs were the Natchez Indians for whom the town was named. They too were a proud race and resented the encroachment of the white man. In vengeance, they massacred nearly three hundred settlers at Fort Rosalie on November 28, 1729, which the French explorer, Jean Baptiste le Moyne, Sieur de Bienville, had named for the Duchess of Pontchartrain and had established some thirteen unlucky years previously. That action proved equally unlucky for the Natchez. A short time later other French soldiers enlisted the aid of the neighboring Choctaws and returned to eliminate the Natchez as a tribe.

The French fleur-de-lis was only the first

of five different flags that were to wave over this riverbank town. At the close of the French and Indian War in 1764, down the river came the British Redcoats. They took over Fort Rosalie renaming it Fort Panmure. During the next ten years English families moved in, some fifteen of them, to occupy large grants of land about the settlement, but at this time the Spanish were in New Orleans and while England was occupied with the rebellious colonists along the Atlantic seaboard, the Spaniards moved up the river and planted their Bourbon banner on the bluff. For nineteen years they stayed with a succession of governors which began in 1779 when Bernardo de Galvez, Governor of New Orleans, took settlement for Spain. He garrisoned the fort in 1781. The last Spanish official, one Don Esteban Minor, was actually an adventurous soldier of fortune from Pennsylvania whose English name was Stephen Minor. It was during this period that Collel, the engineer, designed the town so that today the Spanish influence remains in the heart of the city.

During the American Revolution, the Spanish had helped the Colonists and thought they were helping themselves by driving the British from along the Gulf Coast, so one can imagine their surprise and discomfiture when Andrew Ellicott, an American surveyor of Quaker denomination, arrived on February 24, 1797. President Washington had appointed him as commissioner to determine the boundary, the 31st degree parallel, separating the territories of Spain and those of the new American republic. Although the Treaty of San Lorenzo in 1795 specified that the parallel some thirty-eight miles south of Natchez would mark the line, the Spanish official, Don Manuel Gayoso de Lemos, acting upon orders of Governor

Carondelet in New Orleans, tried various ruses to delay evacuation in hope that the American mission would become weary and retire upstream. Mr. Ellicott, it turned out, was adamant, a man with a purpose, and after raising the United States' flag on the hill behind *Connelly's Tavern,* incited the pro-American element of the town to a point where Governor Gayoso decided that discretion was the better part of valor and modified his efforts. The news that he had been appointed governor of Louisiana undoubtedly fell quite pleasantly upon the ears of Gayoso, and he left leaving Colonel Esteban Minor in charge. It was not until almost a year later however, in March of 1798, that the garrison troops filed from the fort. The Spaniards never returned.

Fort Rosalie was just about all the French left to be remembered by, for during their occupation no serious settlement was attempted, but the English had been there long enough to raise families, and the Spanish had been there long enough to raise buildings as well. *Bontura, Cherokee, Airlie, Cherry Grove, Cottage Gardens, Elgin, Hope Farm, The Elms, King's Tavern, Holly Hedges, Linden, Richmond, Springfield, Routhland, Windy Hill,* and of course, *Connelly's Tavern,* all date back at least in part to the latter days of the eighteenth century and are predominantly late Spanish or early American. Another residence, *Concord,* which burned in 1901 and whose forlorn steps and columns until recent times could be seen near the corner of Gayoso and LaSalle Streets, was erected in 1794 for the genial Gayoso de Lemos. As a structure it appeared distinctly more imposing than its contemporaries and was almost an archetype of the mansions that were soon to follow. It is not too surprising that Winthrop Sargent, the first territorial governor of Mississippi, who was later to acquire the redoubtable *Gloucester,* moved in when Gayoso moved out. It is further interesting to note that Stephen Minor, who stayed on to become an American citizen, bought *Concord* from Sargent in 1808.

The departure of the Spanish marked the beginning of a new era in Natchez for with the advent of the nineteenth century came an influx of Americans down the Natchez Trace from Nashville. The Trace, until this time, was little more than an old buffalo path that the shaggy animals had beaten into the soft loess soil on their way to salt licks or drinking water. Hernando de Soto, whose grave the Mississippi River eventually became, described these paths in 1540 as worn deep into the earth. Several of the trails the Choctaw, Chickasaw, and Natchez tribes had joined together to provide communication among themselves, and this rude system afforded the white pioneers an overland route to the lower Mississippi. In 1801 the remaining tribes signed a treaty with the U. S. Government allowing it to open the Trace as a wagon road over which the mail might travel.

During the next thirty-five years or so this road, often referred to as "the Devil's Backbone," was to serve many a pioneer going west and many a raft, skiff, or a floatboat crew walking back home from New Orleans, for it was difficult to pole upstream on Old Man River. Perhaps at no other time in our history has such a region been dominated by the outlaw. Gangs of cut-throat robbers took over this thoroughfare, and in most cases even the rough rivermen were no match for the likes of Joseph Hare, Samuel Mason, John Murrell, Harry Cranshaw and the brothers, Micajah and Wiley Harpe, the latter known respectively but unaffectionately as Big and Little Harpe. Many of these public enemies, nevertheless, donated their heads as decorations for poles along the Trace, grisly reminders that sometimes crime did not pay.

The Trace as a vital artery to the Southwest began to lessen in importance as early as 1811; for it was late in that year that the first steamboat came down the Ohio and Mississippi Rivers. Not the least of the significant aspects of that journey was the first steamboat cargo on the Mississippi: cotton loaded at Natchez and shipped by some plucky planter to New Orleans on Nicholas J. Roosevelt's slate-blue, two-masted, $38,000 side-wheeler which bore the name of her Louisiana destination. The *New Orleans,* pioneer of the big river, proved conclusively that steam power could navigate the current upstream as well as down thus ushering in an era that would see cotton bring to Natchez the fabulous wealth that was to raise the Greek temples in the green oaks. The first decade of the new century which preceded steam power on the river did bring a few important structures such as *Gloucester, Elmscourt,* the front of *Cherokee, Mistletoe, Pleasant Hill, Jefferson College,* and quite probably the early section of *Green Leaves.* Quite possibly *Glenfield, Propinquity,* or even *The Briers,* whose dates are rather indefinite, belong to this period. With the exception of *Gloucester,* which Governor Sargent remodeled sometime in 1808 or after, none of these buildings could boast of the classic portico which was destined to become the trademark of the cotton kings. It is an interesting fact that at one time Natchez stood second in the country only to New York City in the number of millionaires. It is to them and to Mr. Roosevelt and his steamboat that we are indebted.

By way of contrast, Natchez Under-the-Hill should be mentioned. Even in the days of the rafts and keelboats this miserable strip of land under the bluffs was a spawning ground for river pirates and highwaymen, and it was not uncommon for the crew of a passing vessel to find that they were being shot at just for the fun of it. The inhabitants of this rough little settlement were so vile and murderous that up in Natchez proper the good citizens were forced to dig a moat down the middle of what is now Canal Street and install drawbridges which were drawn each night to keep that less desirable part of the populace where it belonged, under the hill. Silver Street and Water Street, two outrageously sordid thoroughfares lined with brothel and gambling hall, were where gun and dirk ruled with alacrity, and many were the unfortunates who received free trips downstream minus their money and their lives. It was hell on earth then, but today's tourist will probably be just a bit disappointed to find that Water Street has now also gone downstream, and that Silver Street is just a handful of innocuous old buildings dreaming in the warmth of the afternoon sun.

The steamboat era served only to intensify the baseness of that little city blow the bluffs, but at the same time it helped immeasurably to create the magnificence above. By 1830, a date that most authorities consider the beginning of the Classical Revival period, such prominent homes as *Auburn, Arlington, Hawthorne, Belvidere, Mount Repose, Monmouth, Rosalie, The Towers, Twin Oaks,* and possibly *Myrtle Terrace,* a "Mississippi Planter" type which was fairly well restricted to this earlier period, were

built. This last mentioned house eventually, in 1854, became the residence of Captain Thomas P. Leathers whose steamer, *Natchez,* just one of a long series of his gaudily painted boats to bear the name, brought him undying fame from its race with the *Robert E. Lee.* Some of his supporters have clouded this legend with patriotism claiming that Leathers purposely held back so as not to sully the name of the great Southern war hero with another defeat, but others have insisted that doughty old Captain Tom had just as much or more pride in the name of his town and his boat.

Regardless of the *true* facts, the race of the *Lee* and the *Natchez* is an entrancing story like many another that emanated from the big stream, and although it is difficult in many cases to separate fact from fiction, that does not hold true in the case of the *Jim Johnson* or the *E. Jenkins* which were so large that they required hinges and joints to make the bends in the river. The *Jim Johnson* had a smokestack so tall that after they killed the boiler fire in the fall, the smoke was still coming out in the spring, and if that does not sound impressive, maybe the horse racing track around the base of the stack does. Not to be outdone, friends of the *E. Jenkins* insisted she operated a railroad complete with trains, both passenger and freight, atop her deck's guardrails, and that the *Jenkins* mounted a spotlight so powerful that on the darkest night one could see the Capitol at Baton Rouge all the way from Natchez.

One delightful river tale that seems a bit more believable has to do with a certain Captain Russell, master of the good steamboat, *Constellation,* which had been tied up for the night at Natchez Under-the-Hill. One of the captain's paying guests had gone ashore, it seems, to take in the sights and had been taken, and after returning aboard ship where he convinced his host that he had been robbed, the captain himself went ashore to the notorious house which happened to be immediately opposite the boat. There in no uncertain terms he requested that the occupants return the stolen pocketbook and its contents. Meeting only with injured innocence, the riverman left with the warning that if they did not produce the money by the time his boat was ready to leave, the house was going to leave with it. Upon summoning his crew of roustabouts, he returned to secure his boat's largest cable around the house and gave the signal for slow speed ahead. When the rope became taut and the house began to creak ominously, out of a window flew the missing pocketbook with its original contents intact.

By 1830 there were scores of riverboats filled with paying guests sailing the Mississippi for business or for pleasure. It was *the* luxurious mode of travel of the time. During the next thirty years many a Natchez planter sent his family or his cotton, or both, down river to New Orleans and returned with pride and satisfaction to his white-pillared mansion. The era of opulence had begun in earnest. It lasted until what many Southerners refer to as "The War Between the States" occurred. Sometime between Fort Sumter and Appomattox, King Cotton was forced into abdication, and although he was to return eventually, never again did he attain his one-time monumental peak of affluence. While he was at the height of his grandeur though, he gave us a magnificent heritage of houses all through the South but particularly here at Natchez. *Stanton Hall, D'Evereux, Dunleith, Lansdowne, Melrose, Monteigne, Oakland, Ravenna, Weymouth Hall, The Parsonage, Melmont, Edgewood, Glenwood, Choctaw, The Burn, Belmont, Brandon Hall,* and that splendid yet unfinished spectacle, *Longwood,* were all created during those fabulous three decades. That they have survived for us to enjoy is a thankful miracle, for fire or windstorm or indifference have in some instances taken their toll. Fortunately for us too, war and reconstruction and hard times did not prevail over many of those who built them and loved them, or those who inherited them and cherished them. The people who reside in them today have much of that same indomitable spirit and pride in the family name. When you meet these people, you will find them to be genial, courteous, sentimental, and lovable. You will also find that they have backbone, their own ideas and their own customs; and should you see them stand at the playing of "Dixie," do not be too surprised. It's an old tradition down South.

Although much has been written about the people of Natchez and their homes, very seldom are included the interesting little sidelights around town, places that are easily accessible and which can add much to the historic flavor one seeks. For example, at the foot of Main Street atop the river bluff is found a marker which indicates that this particular spot was the southernmost terminal of the famed Natchez Trace. From just a few steps away the view across the river to the lowlands of Louisiana reveals the remnants of the bloody sandbar of Vidalia where early Natchezians settled their differences with sword or dueling pistol. Jim Bowie himself once fought at that very place; however, it was his famous knife which saved him there. Then looking up the river still from the same spot, one sees at the bend on the Mississippi side, the location of the "Devil's Punchbowl." This great hollow in the bluffs which some say was caused by a falling meteorite was once a hideout for river pirates, highwaymen, and runaway slaves. A weirdly beautiful area, it may be reached by traveling up Cemetery Road for about a mile. On your way there, just across from *Weymouth Hall,* you will discover the Natchez Cemetery which can provide the visitor with a most interesting half hour or so of history for here are buried many of the former inhabitants of the houses within these pages. The tombs, the statuary, and the ironwork are certainly worthy of examination.

Many a tourist in his anxiety to reach a certain ante-bellum house has passed right by several pre-war churches of much interest and beauty. The *First Presbyterian* at Pearl and State Streets is a Greek Revival dating from 1829 and designed by Levi Weeks of Boston, the architect of *Auburn.* The Gothic *St. Mary's Cathedral* at Union and Main, a most imposing edifice, was completed in 1842. It succeeded the *Church of San Salvador,* a little chapel of the Spanish period that once stood on Commerce Street between Main and Franklin. It is worth noting that as early as 1698 two Canadian priests arrived here to found missions among the Natchez Indians. French maps indicate a church on the bluffs in 1729, the year that the Natchez went on the warpath against the whites, and a priest, Father Poissons, was listed among the victims of that massacre. Old records refer to a Spanish chapel near Fort Rosalie that was built sometime before the Church of San Salvador.

Another fine church is the *Trinity Episcopal* at Washington and Commerce; it was constructed about 1822 and contains a small slave gallery. In Audubon's landscape at *Melrose,* this building may be identified by a large dome, a feature which is no longer in evidence as it was demolished by the tornado of 1840.

In addition to several other old churches that are easily located and worth more than a passing glance, downtown Natchez can show many ancient buildings such as the *Adams County Courthouse* which rose in 1818 at Wall and State Streets, and at the same location, *Lawyers' Row* built by the Spanish prior to 1796 for probable use as a commissary. Although now a rooming house, this was once the quarters of famous early day attorneys. When the Americans took over from the Spaniards, there was much litigation, and it required the presence of many lawyers at Natchez. The *Parish House of San Salvador* at 311 Market Street is, of course, historic as is the *Governor Holmes House,* also known as the *Conti House,* which was built around 1788 at 207 South Wall. David Holmes was the last territorial governor of Mississippi and the first state governor in 1817.

Many other antique buildings and houses are in evidence, more often than not nameless as well as dateless, but age has a way of showing through in spite of a face-lifting or two, and paint does little to disguise century-old bricks and hand-hewn timbers.

Several short scenic drives near town are rewarding. One in particular begins at *Glenfield,* just off the Lower River Road, and takes the traveler through beautiful back country on the Providence Road past *Providence Plantation* to bring him out on the Old Woodville Road just south of *Gloucester.* Also, another pleasant drive is the restored section of the old Natchez Trace which begins at Cannonsburg, fourteen miles north of Natchez on U. S. Highway 61. This nine-mile segment of the historic pathway, now paved for us moderns, terminates but a brief distance to the east of *Springfield Plantation* where Andrew Jackson was married. Another five miles to the southeast brings one back to U. S. Highway 61 at Fayette. Many other vine-covered, deep-banked roads invite the curious and are alluring, has one the time, for the Natchez country has a certain beauty and a certain remoteness that are not found elsewhere.

It is, of course, impossible in a single volume to include everything of importance about the houses of Natchez. Space limitations prevent the presentation of much family history, truly a completely fascinating subject in itself. This book, however, is rather triadic in design: a pictorial, a reference, and a guide book. A great deal is still to be discovered by the visitor to Natchez, and when some object takes his fancy, he will wonder why, and very understandably, that it was not mentioned. Practically all of these homes have a full complement of storied items and valuable antiques, many literally priceless. For that reason the author had long ago come to think of Natchez as a "museum city" reflecting the charm of the "old South."

For the benefit of those who find it impossible ever to reach Natchez during Pilgrimage time in March, it may be of interest to them to learn that about a dozen and a half Pilgrimage houses are open for a nominal fee during the balance of the year. *Auburn,* in Duncan Park, is open all year around free of charge.

For those interested especially in the flowers, during azalea time which more often than not coincides with the Pilgrimage, some of the most luxuriant gardens include: *Hope Farm, Ravenna, Green Leaves, The Elms, The Burn, Elgin, Melrose, Arlington, The Towers,* and *Monteigne.*

One final recommendation, and this is only to the Pilgrimage time visitor, is the Confederate Pageant. It will be found colorful and exciting and particularly to those who know something of the history of Natchez. Your performers will be the citizens of this town and their sons and daughters. Their talents, their costumes, and their gowns blend charmingly to create a nostalgic atmosphere as each historic tableau unfolds before you, and you will live a little bit back in the old days when the South was young, when life was more graceful, and when hearts were light and gay.

And now, come with me to Natchez!

ROBERT GORDON PISHEL

Linden's celebrated doorway

The Pilgrimage Houses

Airlie, reposing in the seclusion of its well-shaded grounds, tops a breeze-swept rise at the end of Myrtle Avenue. The central approach, a brick walk lined with white iris and a row of ancient cedars leads to what is considered by many authorities the oldest residence in Natchez. It is known to antedate 1790.

Wooden pegs and tongue-groove method hold together many of the timbers of this galleried Spanish Colonial type. The rough-hewn, mortised beams, and the small-paned windows with their handmade blinds testify to the age of *Airlie* and the skill of its early builders.

It is considered quite probable that an early section of the house dates back to near 1775 while the British were at Natchez. It is known to have been owned by Don Jose Vidal, a Spanish captain, Secretary and Interpreter for the District. Later Don Esteban Minor, a Pennsylvania Britisher and soldier of fortune, lived here and after acquiring *Concord,* sold *Airlie* to Daniel Clark, father of Myra Clark Gains, famous New Orleans woman.

One Colonel Steele, a secretary for the Mississippi Territory, lived at *Airlie* and died there in 1802, after which for many years it was known as "the old Buckner home," owned by Judge Aylette H. Buckner of English descent who had journeyed to Natchez by horseback from Virginia. Changing professions, Buckner became one of the leading planters here, and had gathered building materials for a new mansion to be erected near *Airlie*. Like many another planter's dream, his too was shattered. After the fall of Vicksburg, he was to see occupying Federal troops confiscate those materials for use in the construction of a fort erected near-by upon the site of Frank Surget II's splendorous *Clifton* which had been destroyed supposedly for that purpose. *Airlie* was commandeered also and used as a hospital for Northern soldiers whose blood stained its floors.

The War Between the States ruined the fortunes of Buckner, and *Airlie* passed into the hands of Ayres P. Merrill. His descendants, Mr. Linton Merrill and the Misses Mary and Margaret Merrill, own and occupy the house today.

Heirlooms of interest include unusually fine silver, china of Old English and Rose Du Barry patterns, early mahogany and rosewood furniture, and portraits of Frank Surget and Sir William Dunbar.

Airlie

Before 1790

Yankee blood once stained its floors

Arlington, one of the earliest mansions, was built at the east end of Main Street by the widow of Captain James Hampton White, the former Jane Surget, during the period, 1816-1819. Being a daughter of the prominent Frenchman, Pierre Surget, she engaged a Philadelphia architect-contractor to construct it of materials imported from Holland and France as well as costly English brick. A grand ball was held to christen the house, but for Jane White it was her first and last there. She was found dead in her bed the following morning. If she was murdered by one of her servants after the theft of her diamond necklace, a tale that has persisted, there has never been any evidence to authenticate such a story. It is true, however, that the reason for her death was never agreed upon.

The facade is reminiscent of *Gloucester* with its modified Tuscan columns (which some authorities consider Roman Doric), but the plan is entirely different with its full length halls and four rooms on each floor. Downstairs the broad hallway seventeen and one-half feet in height resembles an art museum with its Italian and French masterworks, and the "Gold Drawing Room" to the right of the front entrance is a connoisseur's delight with its many priceless pieces. The sunlight satin damask curtains held with tie-backs of white opaline glass grapes upon gilded bronze grape leaves dominate this golden room. The adjoining library holds in its Gothic bookcases some 8,000 volumes, including one collection purchased in England about 1840 by a former *Arlington* owner, Judge Samuel S. Boyd.

The music room at the left front with its crystal chandelier, family portraits, and ancient spinet, also contains one of three early Natchez harps, and the dining room at the left rear with its rare crystal and china exhibits two noteworthy silver services, one an old American bearing the date 1810 and the other made by Tallois of Paris. From this room through a window with its Gibbs doors, one enters an enclosed back veranda. Here a part of an antique doll collection numbering nearly one thousand, and a most colorful antique glassware display may be enjoyed.

The grounds of *Arlington* are noted for their beauty; a boxwood maze, camellia japonicas, one over twenty feet tall, and the imported shell-pink "Arlington" azaleas lend greatly to the enchantment.

Arlington is the home of Mrs. Hubert Barnum and her daughter, Mrs. Anne Vaughan.

Its builder died on the first night

Arlington

1816-1819

A golden drawing room

Lavishness is the keynote

On the following page: Arlington's antique glass against the sky

The Burn takes its thought-provoking name from the Scotch,
meaning "The Brook." When erected by John P. Walworth,
somewhere around 1835 (exact date unknown), a small stream
crossed the estate to the west where Pearl Street now runs. Shortly
after completion a fire destroyed the second story, and the house
was remodeled into a story-and-a-half cottage of Greek influence.
During the War Between the States, *The Burn* was occupied by
Federal troops. At Pilgrimage time the dining room display is one
of the most outstanding in Natchez. Mr. Sol B. Laub resides here.

Bontura, at 107 South Broadway, stands overlooking the esplanade, the mighty Mississippi River, and the lush lowlands of Louisiana. It is one of the most unique houses in a city noted for its unusual structures.

Before the earliest section of it was built, this land had been the site of the original French settlement, and later the parade grounds during British and Spanish occupations. The alley alongside *Bontura* was once known as Market Street, and although it is not claimed that the arched rear part was erected during the period of French influence, it has been compared to the Old French Market in New Orleans. This part of the dwelling has often been referred to as the Market House as well as the coach or carriage house. It is established that it dates from at least 1790. The central portion seems to have no date, but the picturesque front addition was definitely in place as early as 1832.

Bontura, with its beautiful ironwork, reminds one strongly of the Vieux Carre, the old French Quarter in New Orleans, and its style is often referred to as "Spanish Creole." The L-shape of the house and the adjoining wall to the north form a handsome courtyard whose oleanders, myrtles, and roses create a pleasant "Old World" atmosphere. Bontura possesses more of a European feeling than any other Natchez house because of its obvious age and its narrowness. However, in addition to a parlor, a library, a dining room, and several bedrooms, on the lower floor of the central section there is a ballroom which also doubled as a banquet hall or music room.

Of additional interest is *Bontura's* twenty-foot square basement with its bricked-in door, rather a mysterious room in that such excavations for basements during Spanish days were forbidden.

At one time the property was part of the Tattersalls Stables, but did not receive its present name until 1847 when Don Josef Buntura (it is recorded that this was the correct spelling) purchased the property. Buntura, a wealthy Portuguese wine merchant, had formerly owned the "Natchez Hotel" on Water Street in Natchez Under-the-Hill. A hand-carved cypress bar from just such an establishment may be viewed in the taproom of *Connelly's Tavern.*

During the War Between the States when Natchez was under bombardment from Federal gunboats, a shell from the *U.S.S. Essex* crashed through a door and into a rear wall.

It is claimed that *Bontura* was often host to such important personages as Stephen Foster, Mark Twain, and Captain Tom Leathers of steamboat fame. In early July of 1870, the front galleries were crowded with spectators witnessing the famous race between the *Natchez* and the *Robert E. Lee.*

Choice antiques in a beautifully chosen selection may be found at *Bontura* among which are portraits of George and Martha Washington attributed to Charles Willson Peale, famed artist of revolutionary times.

In 1941 as it was about to be condemned, a providential discovery of *Bontura* occurred; Mr. and Mrs. Hugh Hinton Evans of Los Angeles purchased and restored it with faithful care.

Bontura

1790-1832

Its gallery a box seat for the big race

The Briers is reached only by the use of a long, deep-banked, narrow, twisting road overhung with tree limbs and vines that create an atmosphere of a remote wilderness, yet the house is near town and perched on the river bluff. It is an early planter type whose delightful situation affords a wonderful view of Vidalia and the near-by cotton fields in the Louisiana lowlands.

As a child, Varina Howell, later Mrs. Jefferson Davis, spent many a pleasant moment amusing herself looking out over the river. Although some historians have assumed that she was born at *The Briers,* there seems to be no definite proof that her parents had moved to this house by May 7, 1826, her date of birth. It is known, however, that she lived here until February of 1845 when she became the bride of the man who some sixteen years later was destined to become the President of the Confederacy.

It is not certain who constructed *The Briers* and when, however, it is thought to have been built around 1812 possibly by Peter Little (of *Rosalie*) or his brother-in-law, James S. Griffin, an architect.

There is a great amount of charm to *The Briers.* The wide gallery has three fan-lighted entrances, two of which open into bedrooms.

The third enters the wide central hall off of which is the large dining room on the left and the drawing room on the right. It was before the beautifully carved Adams mantel in this latter room that Jefferson and Varina were married.

At the rear of the house is a very pleasant enclosed veranda; the pillars here are connected in a series of Spanish arches, and at opposing ends of the room mahogany stairways lead to the upper floor. Four bedrooms are upstairs, the central pair of which may be converted into a ballroom by the use of folding doors. This room, also used as a banquet hall, was the scene of the wedding breakfast for Jefferson Davis and his bride.

During the War Between the States, *The Briers* was owned by Walter Irvine and was damaged when a front gallery post was shot away by a Federal gunboat. One of the ship's officers, tradition says, was George Dewey, later to become the famous admiral.

One item of great historic interest to be seen here is the cradle that rocked young Jeff Davis.

In 1927, Mrs. William W. Wall and her late husband bought and with much expense restored *The Briers.*

The Briers

1812

Cherokee, at first glance, seems to be a house of comparatively recent construction, but surprisingly enough it antedates most in Natchez.

There are two sections to the house. The Spanish, now to the rear, was erected in 1794 by Jesse Greenfield on land granted by Don Jose Vidal. It was here in 1798 on the grounds before *Cherokee,* that American troops encamped under the command of Major Isaac Guion who had been sent to reinforce Andrew Ellicott, the surveyor.

In 1810, David Michie, from the family of Michie Tavern fame in Virginia, added the front section. His Natchez tavern, the Michie Hotel near Canal Street on Main, bore the reputation as serving the best food in the territory, but he eventually abandoned the tavern business. After becoming a successful cotton planter, he later became a broker and ship owner. It is thought that his wealth afforded him the services of such an architect as Levi G. Weeks, builder of *Auburn,* who is known to have remodeled several Natchez houses at that time. At any event, the result was something of an early modified Greek Revival with a recessed gallery and built-in, pseudo pediment supported by two simple Doric columns.

The situation of the early part of the house is interesting in that it was built into a hillside in order to avoid an excavation. During the Spanish era any such disturbance of the soil was prevented by law for at that time it was thought that Yellow Fever lurked below ground. The rear section of two stories was only one room wide but quite long; its incorporation with the two-storied front was an architectural triumph that gave Natchez one of its most interesting buildings.

Cherokee has been the residence of several notable families, one of whom was the Frederick Stantons who lived here from 1846 until *Stanton Hall* was completed.

The furnishings are typical of the Natchez Pilgrimage homes; the hand-carved rosewood sofas and chairs, the Aubusson rug, the French gold leaf mirrors, and other pieces of Sheraton and Chippendale do not disappoint the visitor. Of particular note is the painting of General Lafayette at the French Court; and the winding staircase in the early part of the house is a feature of exceptional beauty with its mahogany balustrades and treads with hand-cut ornaments.

Cherokee, perched well above the intersection of Wall and High Streets, is now the residence of Mr. and Mrs. Charles J. Byrne.

An architecture that belies an age

Cherokee

1794-1810

Connelly's Tavern was built about 1795 upon a ridge which was then known as Myrtle Bank. Its elegance leads one to assume that it was constructed as a residence of Creole influence, although one Patrick Connelly leased the place about 1797 for use as a tavern. That same year, the Quaker, Andrew Ellicott, raised the American flag for the first time in this territory. The tavern hill now bears his name.

It is believed that Louis Philippe, then Duke of Orleans but later the last king of France, was entertained here by Major Isaac Guion. It was the presence of Guion and the American troops which he commanded upon Ellicott's Hill that finally persuaded the Spanish to evacuate Fort Rosalie in 1798.

In 1807, Aaron Burr, former Vice-President of the United States who at one time had lost the Presidency to Jefferson by one vote, conspired in a meeting in the *Tavern* with the well-to-do Irish emigrant, Harman Blennerhasset, who was financing Burr's plan to establish a new country carved out of the Southwest. Although the traitor was apprehended, he was never convicted during his trial beneath the now famous oaks at Washington, Mississippi.

In the taproom of the *Tavern* is the very bench upon which Burr was seated during his hearing.

During the early days the lower floor of the *Tavern* was used for the common traveler, the upper for the elite. Four rooms downstairs include the kitchen and the taproom, and upstairs are located the ballroom, a dining room, and two bedrooms. Authorities are convinced that the *Tavern* with its vaulted ceilings and hand-cut timbers was the work of a shipwright. Of singular interest is the rare and beautiful Waterford crystal chandelier recessed in the ceiling of the ballroom.

Actually the building was not used as a tavern for long; it again became a residence for many prominent people including Judge Samuel Brooks who served as the first mayor of Natchez from 1802 until 1811. During the 1840's it was known as the Cornish School, later as the Natchez High School, and still later it had deteriorated into a low-class tenement. When the Natchez Garden Club acquired it for its headquarters in 1935, the *Tavern* was in a deplorable condition, but with the aid of Richard Koch, noted architect of New Orleans, the marvelous restoration of today was accomplished.

High on Ellicott's hill

Connelly's Tavern

1795

Connelly's Tavern

Saved by the Natchez Garden Club

Where Blennerhasset awaited Burr

Connelly's Tavern

Sustenance for the weary traveler

D'evereux, an admirable inheritance from the Greek Revival period, is a classic example of that type.

During a period of many months materials were gathered to insure proper seasoning and preparation for its construction. James Hardy, a prominent architect of the time, built this white brick temple completing it in 1840 for its owner, William St. John Elliot. As in most brick Natchez houses, local clay was utilized.

At the front and rear Hardy placed six fluted Doric columns to support the entablature beneath the hipped roof. The gallery ceiling he paneled and ornamented with medallions, and his majestic creation was crowned with a railed observatory. A further embellishment, a small, fancy ironwork balcony of graceful design surmounted the front entrance, but at the rear a full gallery was placed overlooking a courtyard. For reasons known only to James Hardy, the rear doorway was made far more elaborate than that of the front entrance.

The floor plan consists of the simple four rooms up, four down with dividing hallways. Large double parlors are to the right, and a dining room on the left is separated from a large butler's pantry by a stairwell containing a mahogany-railed, semi-circular stairway that mounts to the third floor. The Greek motif was carried throughout the house, acanthus leaves and Greek Key decorations being in evidence.

Mr. Elliot, a long-time personal friend of Henry Clay, gave in honor of the latter during his Presidential campaign, one of the most magnificent balls ever witnessed in Mississippi, and "The Great Pacificator," as he was called as a result of his conciliations and his *Compromise of 1850,* was often a guest at *D'Evereux.* At one time, an amusing error occurred, perhaps not to Mr. Clay, when a servant mistook the great statesman for a tramp and set the dogs upon him.

Originally the land consisted of eighty acres, and prior to the War Between the States, *D'Evereux* could boast of the most impressive gardens in the vicinity. Twelve of the acres were landscaped, and at the back a series of thickly planted terraces descended to a lake complete with mill, boats, and swans. During reconstruction times following the War, the grounds were used as a camp site for Federal troops, and their beauty destroyed.

Later, *D'Evereux* became a rental property and one farmer tenant not only stabled his horses in hallway and gallery, but even used its rooms for the storage of yams.

Today, the public is indebted to Miss Myra Virginia Smith, its owner, for the fine restoration of *D'Evereux.*

D'Evereux

1840

Dunleith is undoubtedly one of the most picturesque ante-bellum houses in existence. Crowning a pleasant rise just off Homochitto Street at Winchester Road, it is, obviously, a Greek Revival period "temple," but one of exceptional charm and grace. It was completed in 1849 by Charles Dahlgren, a lineal descendant of Gustavus Adolphus, King of Sweden. It is said that Dahlgren, a man with a quick temper, bore the scars of many a duel and carried proudly within his body two pistol balls, mementos of his impetuous courage. During the War Between the States, he gained considerable fame as a Confederate general, and his disputes with President Jefferson Davis over the conduct of the war were so bitter that he never forgave Davis.

The present house was erected on the site of a former classic edifice built by Job Routh, one of the earliest Natchez settlers. He was the son of Jeremiah Routh, a Welsh emigrant who migrated to Mississippi from Virginia after securing a four hundred acre British land grant. The father was driven from his holdings in about 1779 by the incoming Spaniards. In 1847 Job's former residence, known as *Routhlands,* was destroyed by fire after being struck by lightning while the current owners, the Dahlgrens, were away. The entrance steps to the southeast side of *Dunleith* and the stables belonged to old *Routhlands,* the original house whose grounds were part of a seven hundred acre Spanish land grant to the Routh family whose holdings stretched almost fifteen miles along the river. Job, perhaps a bit more crafty than his father, had married Anne Miller, sister of Christopher Miller, secretary to the Spanish government.

The colonnaded galleries of this classic *Dunleith* give rise to the impression that some mansion of a Louisiana sugar planter served as the model. *Greenwood,* built in 1830 near St. Francisville, is quite similar although minus the upper gallery. *Three Oaks,* dating from 1840 and located south of New Orleans, is very reminiscent, and *Oak Alley,* near Vacherie on the Mississippi River, an 1836 creation of George Swainey, the architect, for Alexander Roman, is almost identical with its twenty-eight Doric columns.

A most engaging legend of *Dunleith* concerns a Miss Isabel Percy, a relative of Mrs. Dahlgren's first husband, who came here to live following a broken romance with a member of the court of Louis Philippe of France. Legend says her mournful voice and harp are heard each twilight as the ghostly fingers of Miss Percy pass softly over the strings.

Dunleith is the home of Mr. and Mrs. N. Leslie Carpenter.

Like a Louisiana sugar planter's

Dunleith

1847-1849

Elgin, pronounced with the hard "g" which was imported from Scotland, is located some six miles south of town. The earliest part of the house, to the rear, was erected sometime around 1780; its smallish, low-ceilinged rooms indicate Spanish origin. The builder is not known, but the land had been part of a grant from Spain to William Dunbar, an early prominent citizen of Natchez. This grant was made by the Spanish government as a reward for his services as a surveyor in this district. Although known as "Sir William," Dunbar never returned to his home "Elgin," in Morayshire, Scotland, to claim the title which he could have rightly inherited.

The double-galleried front portion with its ninety-foot width was added in 1840 by Dr. John Carmichael Jenkins who had inherited the estate from his uncle, Dr. John F. Carmichael. Sentimentally, Dr. Jenkins and his bride, the former Annis Dunbar whom he had met at *The Forest,* her near-by ancestral home, named the newly remodeled residence, "Elgin," in honor of her grandfather, Sir William. The clay and timber of the plantation were fashioned by slave labor into the materials used in *Elgin's* construction. Even the punkah in the dining room was made on the plantation cut from one oaken plank. An interesting feature of the fenestration is the use of the Gibbs door beneath each window opening on both galleries. These small doors, at floor level, give maximum ventilation.

Dr. Jenkins, a scientist who among other things raised fowls and birds for cross breeding purposes, became nationally known as a horticulturist whose experiments in fruit grafting rivaled those of Luther Burbank's of this century. He was one of the first scientists to come to the conclusion that soil was exhaustible and that it must receive fertilization and be allowed to lie fallow at intervals. Another indication of his brilliance was his inspiration to ship early fruit in ice to New York markets by steamboat. His genius was lost in the Yellow Fever epidemic of 1855 when both he and his wife perished.

Noteworthy furnishings of *Elgin* include one of the very first kerosene lamps to appear in Mississippi, rosewood furniture, thought to be English, which was upholstered in horsehair, and black marble mantels in parlor and library. The Grandfather's clock with its built-in calendar was made by Hadwin of Liverpool, England, in 1720.

Like many another old plantation, *Elgin,* too, has its ghost. A very fitting spirit, a gentlemanly John Jenkins sits by the entrance gate at dusk nodding politely to all who pass.

Elgin is now the residence of Mrs. William S. R. Beane and family.

Elgin Plantation

1780-1840

Elmscourt, although it is now rather difficult to imagine, was originally a colonial type of structure with pillared portico.

The central part of the house is believed to have been erected in 1810 by Lewis Evans, the first territorial sheriff of Mississippi and consequently the first sheriff of Adams County. This original portion was a square, two-story brick building.

About 1851, Evans sold the house to the tremendously wealthy Frank Surget, one of the "golden Surgets" from *Cherry Grove.* Later, Surget gave it as a wedding gift to his daughter, Jane, and her husband Ayres P. Merrill II. Surget was reputed to be one of the three multi-millionaires in the United States at that time. Although the depression of 1837 made paupers of many such Southerners, not so with the wily Frank whose investments were safe in Europe.

Upon receiving *Elmscourt,* the Merrills remodeled it, and the wooden columns and railings were replaced with the exquisite grape design ironwork from Naples. Spacious one-story wings, recessed from the front line of the house, were added and a private gas plant and water works installed. The War Between the States was, of course, an unhappy experience for Ayres Merrill for he was evidently not a secessionist. It has been written that during this period not only was his cotton gin burned by a mob, but a guard had to be posted to prevent the destruction of *Elmscourt.* He weathered it though, and after establishing a strong friendship with General Ulysses S. Grant whom he entertained frequentley here, found himself appointed United States Minister to Belgium when Grant became President.

Later on, Ayres P. Merrill, Jr. sold *Elmscourt* to another Surget, James, who gave it in turn to his daughter, Carlotta, upon her marriage to David McKittrick. It was during the ownership of this latter pair that the many candelabra, wall sconces, and crystal chandeliers found throughout *Elmscourt* gave inspiration for the famed "Ball of a Thousand Candles" which was a feature for several years of the early Natchez Pilgrimages.

Among the many fine furnishings here is an English serving table, carved in black snake design of the Cavendish family, bearing coat-of-arms of the Duke of Devonshire. White Italian marble mantels are carved with grape design to match the exterior ironwork.

The Robert E. Honnolls now occupy *Elmscourt* which is the property of Mrs. Grace McKittrick McNeil.

Elmscourt

1810

Fancy ironwork from Italy

The Elms, another of the double-galleried early Spanish type, was erected sometime around 1783 when this territory was a Spanish province. The house is a large two and one-half story rambling structure galleried on three sides and set well back within the deep shade of oaks. It is believed elm trees once there gave origin to its name. Interesting features include a lacy, circular, wrought-iron stairway, formerly on the exterior, thought to be a Portuguese import, and a set of call bells with different rings for each servant. Long known as "the old Drake home," *The Elms* and its beautiful gardens now belong to Mrs. Joseph Kellogg, a descendant of Moseley J. P. Drake.

44   On Opposite Page: Green Leaves' garden

Green Leaves, nestled in the deep shade of ancient live oaks that spread their gnarled limbs in great sweeps, has witnessed the march of the decades since the early 1800's.

Its original owner or builder is unknown, but undoubtedly part of the house antedates the War of 1812. This location was a square of Williamstown, a subdivision, before the Battle of New Orleans and was purchased by Jonathan Thompson. It is quite probable that he erected the original house at that time. The tragic story of his family took place during a Yellow Fever epidemic in May of 1820 when he and his wife, Anna, and their three children all died within a few days from the dread disease.

In 1849, *Green Leaves* was sold by Edward Fourniquet to George Washington Koontz, and about a year later it was remodeled into the raised cottage type complete with small, Grecian Doric-columned front portico. Koontz was a personal friend of the Confederate President, and during the war was commissioned by Davis to make trips to Europe to negotiate loans for the Confederacy.

A memento of the Reconstruction period following the great North-South struggle may be observed in the overhead glass of the doorway. Pillagers, posing as soldiers, rode the streets, and one outlaw fired upon Mr. Koontz but missed. The bullet hole is evidence.

The front entrance at *Green Leaves* opens into a large hall which divides the double drawing rooms on the left from the dining room and bedrooms to the right. At the rear of the front section, two galleried wings join at right angles to form one of the most beautiful courtyards in the vicinity. Flagstoned walks, bird bath, and exquisite plants including azaleas and flowering dogwood are canopied by a huge live oak whose circumference measures more than thirteen feet. Legend tells us that this tree has lived over three hundred years and that formerly the Natchez Indians held their councils or "pow-wows" beneath its spreading branches.

Rosewood furniture, bronze chandeliers, black marble mantels, great mirrors, rare gold leaf vases, historic souvenirs of the War Between the States, and many other praiseworthy items are seen at *Green Leaves*. Perhaps the greatest attraction is the set of rare china, each unduplicated piece decorated with bird or flower design. The artist may well have been John James Audubon; many authorities consider the work to resemble that of the great naturalist very closely, although it is unsigned.

Green Leaves is the home of Mrs. Ruth Audley Beltzhoover and family.

Green Leaves

Before 1812

Gloucester, situated just off the Old Woodville Road, is one of the very earliest mansions of the Natchez district.

Most authorities agree that it was erected in 1799 or thereabouts by David Williams or his family. According to a deed, both Nathaniel Tomlinson and Samuel Young owned the house, then known as "Bellevue," before Abijah Hunt sold it to Winthrop Sargent on May 30, 1808, for twenty thousand dollars. At that time it was the center of a five thousand acre cotton plantation although the house was not then in its present form.

Sargent, the first territorial governor of Mississippi, not only changed the name of the house to honor his home town back in Massachusetts, but in remodeling *Gloucester,* it is said, doubled the width which necessitated a second front entrance for balance. Obviously the imposing Grecian portico with its galleries and pediment supported by modified Roman Doric columns necessarily would have been added at that time. A five columned back gallery on the south and the dry moat which encompasses three sides of the house were further inspirations of Mr. Sargent or his architect.

The basement or ground floor of *Gloucester* is something uncommon with its heavily barred windows and doors, and one authority indicates that four of the seven rooms therein were

for the storage of wines. This might have been so, but they say that Winthrop Sargent had brought his New England Puritanism along; it found him in conflict with many of the easy-going ways of the South.

On the first floor of *Gloucester* the twin entrances open into a U-shaped hall which surrounds the library. At each side of this room are twin stairways thought to resemble those of the old Sargent home in Massachusetts. Two end rooms on this floor, the dining room at the left and the drawing room on the right, have peculiar "octagonal" shaped walls. Two small rooms back of these open also upon the rear gallery. On the second floor are three bedrooms.

During the Federal occupation of Natchez, Winthrop's son, George Washington Sargent, was murdered at the front door one night by pillaging Union soldiers who were later captured, tried, and executed on the grounds of *D'Evereux.*

The furnishings here are outstanding. Much fine china and silver, many valuable paintings by old masters, rare first editions in the library, and mantels of black African and Italian marble are especially memorable.

Gloucester is the residence of Mrs. Lenox Stanton.

A Puritan remodeled it

Gloucester

About 1799

Hawthorne, like many another Southern Planter type cottage, is deceptively spacious. Double front doors open upon a grand hallway whose four fanlighted doorways are in themselves architecturally rare, but the true delight of *Hawthorne* is its immaculate rosewood, mahogany, brocades, and crystal. It is generally accepted that Jonathan Thompson, step-son-in-law of Governor Sargent, built the house in 1814; however, its location was originally part of a large British grant to the Williams family. Tradition says Lafayette visited here in 1825. Excellently restored by the McGehee family, *Hawthorne* is now owned by Mrs. Carl A. McGehee.

On following page: The beauty of a Hawthorne bedroom

Hope Farm, screened from public view by luxuriant plantings at the junction of Duncan Avenue and Homochitto Street, is one of the oldest residences in Natchez.

The older part of this historic house is the eight-room two-story wing at the back. This pleasant, double-galleried structure standing above terraced gardens was erected during the English period of Natchez by Marcus Hailer in 1775 or before. Don Carlos de Grand-Pre, a French adventurer who became a Spanish governor in 1789, bought *Hope Farm* that same year and added the typically Spanish front portion. Seven hand-hewn cypress columns support the low sweeping roof forming a broad gallery that overlooks the front terraces which have long been noted for their massive floral beauty.

Indicative of its age and origin, the front entrance opens directly into a large living room rather than a hallway. Sliding doors connect this room with the dining room to the left; the kitchen is to the rear from the dining room. A den behind the living room opens onto a raised back gallery, Louisiana French in flavor. On the south, two bedrooms complete this section of the house. Ceilings here are low indicating the Spanish influence.

When Governor Grand-Pre enlarged *Hope Farm,* he retained the English wing with its kitchen, dining, and bedroom facilities for over-night guests. The charming bedrooms here are still used for that purpose as the present owners extend their hospitality to the Natchez Pilgrim. One such room, illustrated in this book, offers twin, apple-wood, canopied beds that were made on a plantation.

The fourteen rooms of *Hope Farm* are most attractively furnished with many valuable and admirable antiques; the six-octave mahogany piano of the living room, a set of century old china, and a rare crystal lamp in the dining room are but a few of the owners' treasures. Several items of historic interest include a bell and the carved Indian figurehead from the steamboat, *Natchez.*

During early spring, red, white, pink, and purple azaleas line the walks of the back gardens, and dogwood, tulips, and other flowers transform the rear terraces into a sight delightful to behold.

Hope Farm belonged to the Montgomery family for ninety years, but in 1927 it was purchased by the J. Balfour Millers and authentically restored. The eminent Mrs. Miller, the former Katherine Grafton, is a descendant of an old Natchez family whose earliest arrival was Daniel Grafton in 1763. She, more than anyone, was responsible for the success of the first Pilgrimage in 1932; many a Natchez residence standing today owes its very existence to her courage and efforts.

One of Natchez's very oldest

Hope Farm

1775-1789

Dining room at Pilgrimage time

Bedroom in the English wing

On following page: Azalea gardens at Hope Farm

Holly Hedges, previously known as "Carson Cottage," situated at the corner of Washington and South Wall Streets, was re-named and beautifully restored by Mr. and Mrs. Earl Hart Miller. A Don Juan Scott received permission from the Spanish authorities to construct the house in 1795, the Spaniards stipulating facetitiously, however, that no bull fights could be held in the yard. It was remodeled after the Greek influence in 1832 by the John T. McMurrans (later of *Melrose*) who received it as a wedding gift from her father, Judge Edward Turner who had bought it in 1818. *Holly Hedges'* fascinating furnishings include much scenic wallpaper and many priceless antiques.

Linden is another of the early Spanish houses which have been enlarged at various times, until they finally reached impressive proportions.

The central portion of this house was the original part consisting of four large rooms and hallways, two rooms on each floor. As is the case with a great many of the eighteenth century houses, no actual proof exists as to its first owner or builder. Some historians have concluded, however, that *Linden,* as well as *The Elms, Gloucester, Holly Hedges,* and *Connelly's Tavern,* was the work of the builder and shipwright, Don Juan Scott of the Spanish era. It is certain, however, that the house was standing as early as 1790 on a tract consisting of at least one hundred acres upon which a half dozen well known ante-bellum houses are now standing.

In 1818, James Moore sold *Linden* to Thomas B. Reed, the first United States Senator from Mississippi, and it was re-named "Reedland." The Reeds transformed the place into one of Natchez's most admired, widening each side with one story extensions and adding a ninety-eight-foot gallery across the front, employing ten slender carved pillars of solid cypress. To the central portion of the second story was built a much smaller gallery with but four columns supporting a light and graceful pediment complete with ovaled window.

Dr. John Ker bought *Linden* in 1829 from the Reeds who had purchased *The Vale,* the site of which is now the Johns-Manville plant on Liberty Road. Dr. Ker, together with his partner, Dr. Stephen Duncan of *Auburn,* spent nearly twelve years fighting the opponents of a mutual friend's will which had stipulated that his slaves be freed. The case of Captain Isaac Ross became a notoriously bitter contest, but in the end and after Ker's death, Ross' wishes were carried out.

In 1840, *Linden* became the property of Mrs. Jane Gustine Conner who gave the house the U-shaped courtyard by the addition of two wings. She also was to give five sons to the Confederacy for which she became known as the "Little War Mother."

Of particular note is the front entrance with its Doric pillars, framed fanlight, and sidelights set in alternating diamond and oval panes. This is perhaps the most celebrated doorway in Natchez.

Linden is the home of Mr. and Mrs. Frank Fauntleroy and Mr. and Mrs. Elliott Trimble. Mrs. Fauntleroy is a great-great-granddaughter of Jane Gustine Conner.

Linden

Before 1790

With a doorway of exceptional charm

Longwood represents a planter's dream that did not quite come true.

Haller Nutt was a cotton planter and son of Dr. Rush Nutt whose scientific experiments with the cotton plant and inventiveness with the cotton gin and compress brought him much acclaim. By 1859, Haller was a man of means and influence and wished for something in the way of a mansion to reflect not only his wealth and prestige but also his own creativeness. By this time the Greek Revival period was pretty well on the wane, and in its place octagonally-shaped houses were beginning to appear, especially in the East. Mr. Nutt took his ideas to the well-known architect, Samuel Sloan, in Philadelphia, and together they devised an eight-sided castle six stories high. Later, some were to call this architecture "Steamboat Gothic." Others termed it Oriental or Moorish, but in the end, most of them referred to the house only as "Nutt's Folly."

It has been said by those who know that Mr. Nutt poured one hundred thousand dollars into his dream, and that was in a day when a dollar really went a long way. To Europe went orders for mantels, and stairways, and statues all of Italian marble. Purchases of fine fabrics, tapestries, satins and laces, and silver were arranged for in Ireland and elsewhere. The brickwork of the house had been erected by Nutt's slaves before Mr. Sloan's craftsmen arrived to put on the frosting: the fancy plaster work, the hardwood flooring and stairways, and the marble work. The Nutt family, living in the small Spanish type structure near by, watched with pride as the grounds with their imported plant-ings and artificial lake shaped up to their expectations. This was April, 1861, and a beautiful month in Natchez.

Then the news arrived. Fort Sumter had been fired upon in Charleston harbor, and the war between the North and the South had begun. Mr. Sloan's men dropped whatever they were doing; they were Yankees and they were going back to Pennsylvania. The irony of fate had manifested itself once more—Haller Nutt was himself a Unionist. Dejectedly the family moved into the basement floor which had been finished, and then in 1863 with his dream still incomplete, Haller Nutt died.

Today, the visitor to *Longwood* sees it just about as it stood on that fateful April day. Scaffoldings, old paint buckets, and other abandoned materials are still in evidence where Mr. Sloan's men left them. One may wander through the unfinished upper floors, past niches where marbles were to stand and into the rotunda where Haller Nutt had meant for an ingenious system of mirrors located high in the tower to light this gloomy interior.

Outside, vacancies where marble steps were to have appeared are silent mockeries of Nutt's folly, as is the glassless tower with its giant cupola whose tall wooden spire long ago fell prey to woodpeckers.

Longwood is still in the hands of Nutt's heirs. Three are grandchildren who live out of state, the fourth, Mrs. Agnes Marshall Ward of *Lansdowne,* is the widow of the late James Haller Ward, a grandson of *Longwood's* builder.

A Moorish castle deep in the forest

Longwood

1861

Lansdowne, named in honor of an Englishman, the Marquis of Lansdowne, was built around 1853.

George M. Marshall I and his bride, the former Charlotte Hunt, received the land, six hundred acres, as a wedding gift from her father, David Hunt. Known as "King David" because of his immense wealth, he could hardly miss one plantation when he owned a total of twenty-five with an aggregate of seventeen hundred slaves to tend them.

Fully appreciative of their gift, George Marshall and his wife set forth to build themselves a plantation home commensurate with their extensive holdings of cotton land. They kept in mind the possibility that their future needs might dictate something more on the order of a mansion, so upon a heavy foundation a simple floor plan included double walls and double-flued chimneys. Should they need another story, there would be little trouble involved in its addition. For some obscure reason, the Marshalls never got around to that second story, but they had every right to be proud of their home.

The visitor at *Lansdowne* today sees it pretty nearly as it was in 1853. Stepping into the drawing room, from the fifteen-foot wide hallway one steps into the middle of the last century; the double set of French rosewood furniture covered in rose brocade, the Aubusson carpet, the gilded cornices, and the brocatelles, combine to give the room a rose gold effect. Especially interesting items of this drawing room include the original hand-painted French wallpaper of floral design, and one of Natchez's most beautiful mantels. The latter, an imported white marble ornament, is decorated with an unusual carved calla lily design. The handsome bronze chandelier originally burned the fuel that emanated from *Lansdowne's* own coal-gas plant, the first such private system in Mississippi.

Among the many appealing items of this fine old plantation house are black Egyptian marble mantels in the bedrooms, much fine glass and silver, many rosewood bedroom furnishings, and a quantity of antique art objects.

One historically outstanding attraction is the remains of a huge set of Du Barry china with delicate apricot banding. This the first Mrs Marshall was able to recover from the road where it had been discarded by marauding Union soldiers who had stolen it from her home.

Lansdowne is now the residence of Mr. and Mrs. George M. Marshall III and Mrs. Agnes Marshall Ward.

Only one of twenty-five plantations

Lansdowne

1853

Just like a century ago

Mistletoe belongs to that type of architecture known as "Mississippi Planter" with its full front gallery and sloping roof. Erected about 1807 for young Peter Bisland and his bride, Barbara Foster, it was a wedding gift of the well-known John Bisland, Peter's father whose plantation, "Mount Airwell," stood directly opposite across the old Selsertown road. *Mistletoe* is small, simple, and sturdy with hand-sawed timbers and wooden pegs indicating its age. Its antique furnishings are of great interest and include portraits by James Reid Lambdin and the notable Hall portrait of "Helen" whose physical charms a prim young lady retouched out of modesty. *Mistletoe* is owned by Mr. and Mrs. Jeff Lambdin.

Melrose, it has often been said, could very well serve as the perfect model for the Southern ante-bellum mansion. The house, grounds, and furnishings have seen little change since the middle 1840's when the John T. McMurrans built it. When the steamer *Fashion* burned near Baton Rouge in 1866, Mr. McMurran gained the unhappy distinction of becoming the most prominent Natchez citizen ever to lose his life in a riverboat disaster.

Melrose stands in landscaped grounds neat as an English park, one feature of which is a large, glassy pool shaded with cypress, a tree not common to this immediate vicinity. The architecture of the house might be termed Georgian except for its Classical Revival details such as the massive portico with its smooth Doric columns. The clean lines of its facade are further accentuated by the low, wide steps. Added perfection are the precise yet attractive ironwork railings and the exactness of the mortaring in the brickwork.

The twin drawing rooms of *Melrose* are resplendent. The front, with its green-gold effect from draperies and upholstered rosewood, contains what was known a century ago as a game chair whose seats swivel; the adjoining rose-gold room with black Egyptian marble mantel and crystal-tiered chandelier vies with its neighbor in elegance.

The dining room, which presents an exhibit of Melrose silver, a pattern designed to reflect the splendid dignity of the house for which it was created, is dominated by the most elaborately carved punkah in town. A servant pulling a cord swung this red mahogany fan to create a breeze. (Other fine examples of the punkah may be observed at *Linden, Longwood, Elgin,* and *Elmscourt.*)

Another important attraction of the dining room is the landscape of Natchez by John James Audubon, quite probably the only such painting of its type ever done by the renowned naturalist. While he was in and around Natchez collecting birds and studying oil painting with John Steen, a wandering artist, he also gave children drawing, dancing, and voice lessons. At that time a local matron commissioned Audubon to paint a panoramic view of the town; but she suddenly died, and her family would not accept the work. The artist offered it for sale elsewhere, and finally Emile Profilet, a French citizen of Natchez, bought it at a bargain price and sent it to his European relatives because his shop could be seen therein. Shortly before the Civil War, Profilet visited in France and brought the landscape back with him, although it never elicited any particular acclaim and became "lost." Luckily, George M. Davis, who purchased *Melrose* in 1865, located and was able to re-acquire this rare painting for Natchez years later.

Another much admired item of *Melrose* is its circular shaped table inlaid with delicately hued marbles forming bird designs, the jeweled eyes of which were picked out, tradition says, by Union soldiers.

The back of *Melrose* with its long galleries and columns is also quite attractive. Here an oak-shaded rear court is formed by outer buildings which are not connected to the house. One such structure contains the old kitchen which is still in use, a feature seldom seen today.

Melrose has been the home of Mrs. George M. D. Kelly since 1901.

Here the old South reached its peak

Melrose

1845

Melrose,

Perfection down to the last detail

With red mahogany to stir the air

To complement its neighbor

Melrose

Time stands still amongst its elegance

Monmouth is associated primarily with one of America's early military heroes, General John Anthony Quitman.

In 1821, young Quitman arrived in Natchez from Rhinebeck, New York, to make his fortune in the wealthy cotton district. Although he soon proved his ability as a lawyer and showed definite possibilities as a politician, he exhibited a pronounced fondness of things military. The Natchez Fencibles, a local organization which he formed and drilled as their captain, later became part of his command during the War with Mexico. It was during this conflict that Quitman obtained national acclaim, for as a major general he led his division with brilliance and courage. At Chapultepec, that fortified hill where ancient kings had lived, his men stormed the rocky battlements and captured the Belen Gate which commanded the way into the Mexican capital. Then to cap the climax, Quitman paraded his troops into the Grand Plaza and gave the honor of raising the American flag to Fred Macrery, a Natchez boy.

Upon his return to Mississippi, John Quitman soon found his military reputation to be a great political asset. He became governor of the state although dutifully resigning in 1851 when arrested for a breach of neutrality by reason of his interference in Cuban affairs; he was anti-Spanish to a fault. Later, however, he served in Congress from 1855 to 1858.

Even at his death, drama followed this celebrated Mississippian. At a banquet in Washington for President James Buchanan in 1859, he was among several who were mysteriously poisoned. Always a fighter though, it took many weeks for him to succumb; after returning to Natchez to die in his beloved *Monmouth,* he was buried on the estate. Cities in six Southern states have been named in his honor.

It was often said that *Monmouth* was like the general—handsome in a rugged sort of way, sturdy and simple. The house was built in about 1818 by another New Yorker, the wealthy John Hankinson. His death and that of his wife was another tragic story that occurred when as good Samaritans they found and took into their home a Yellow Fever victim only to fall prey to the disease also.

The portico at *Monmouth* is a bit uncommon for its period in that the pillars are square unlike those of the usual Greek Revival orders; the gallery floor is of slate. Handsome front and rear entrances are identical and noted for their fanlights. The owner, Mrs. Hubert Barnum of *Arlington,* has furnished *Monmouth* from her enormous collection of choice antiques. The table setting of the dining room at Pilgrimage time is especially pleasing with its deep red china pieces. Another item of interest here is a case of stuffed birds collected and mounted by John James Audubon to serve as models for his fabulous paintings.

Monmouth

1818

A hero died within its rugged walls

Monteigne is one of the more elegant houses of Natchez. With its classic white columns, ancient oaks, enormous camellias and azaleas, and formal gardens, it is beautifully distinctive.

Monteigne's most famous owner was its builder, the dashing Confederate major general, William T. Martin. A Kentuckian by birth and of French Huguenot ancestry, the young man arrived in Natchez by steamboat on a trip to New Orleans where he had planned to establish himself. It was late winter by the calendar, but early spring in Mississippi, and the gardens were in full bloom; therefore it is not difficult to understand why he was to cancel the remainder of his voyage and settle here.

Martin's unusual abilities were proved by his early career as a schoolteacher and the fact that he afterward became a district attorney at the age of twenty-two. Following his marriage to Margaret Conner at "Cleremont," a house now known as *Belmont* on Liberty Road, the Martins purchased this acreage to build upon as Margaret's mother had recently acquired the near-by *Linden*. For their homesite they chose a mysteriously cleared spot in the forest, and realized later upon digging for the foundation that a previous structure had stood there. A great hand-hewn piece of timber, probably the remains of a French settler's house which had been destroyed during the massacre of 1729, was discovered. The Martins completed their home at that spot in 1855 and called it *Monteigne,* the French Huguenot name for Martin. This structure was described as a "French Chalet" with a steep roof; its narrow galleries supported with slender columns were connected with delicate wrought iron railings.

An outside stairway led to the upper bedrooms.

Although William T. Martin was a Southerner through and through, he was greatly opposed to secession as he considered the odds too much in favor of the North militarily. However, when war was thrust upon him, he reorganized the Adams County Troop and even traveled to Massachusetts to purchase arms for the South. In the Confederate army he rose from captain to major general serving with the cavalry of J. E. B. Stuart and with "Little Joe" Brown. His reputation as a warrior preceded him home after Appomattox, and he returned to find that occupying Federal troops had taken their revenge out upon *Monteigne*. Not only had the grounds been laid waste, but the interior had been looted and mutilated, the drawing rooms having been used for the stabling of horses.

In recent times, this house was remodeled by the late Leslie N. C. Carpenter, also an owner of *Dunleith. Monteigne,* that was born in the Greek Revival period, finally received the classical treatment with its handsome columns and pediment. The azaleas which border the porch are some of the finest in the district; for the owners, the William J. Kendalls, have long been noted for their interest in that flower as well as the camellia, and many varieties of each may be found here.

Inside, *Monteigne* possesses a beauty equal to that of its grounds. The entrance hall with its black and white mosaic marble floor, its graceful stairway with harp-like balustrade, and the scenic French hand-blocked Zuber wallpaper, is perhaps the most beautiful in all of Mississippi.

Built by a Confederate general

Monteigne

1855

Mount Repose, northeast of town on the Pine Ridge road, is a large, square-columned, double-galleried, many-sectioned house which William Bisland built sometime prior to 1824. The land had been a 1782 Spanish grant of five hundred and fifty-two acres to his father, John Bisland, one of the earliest cotton planters hereabouts. The oak-lined driveway which was never used dates back to 1824 when William Bisland declared he would not use it until Henry Clay became President. The house has been occupied by descendants of the Bisland family ever since. A very interesting item here is a slave-made, cherry wood desk, formerly belonging to Judge W. B. Shields, attorney for Aaron Burr at his trial. *Mount Repose* is the residence of Dr. J. D. Shields.

The Parsonage has undeniably the most amusing history of any Natchez house. Eliza Low, wife of Peter Little of *Rosalie,* acquired the habit of entertaining all visiting ministers who so overran their own home that Mr. Little resolved to house them elsewhere. He built *The Parsonage* near by in 1840. It is a sturdy brick structure with English basement and a high, raised front gallery which faces the river bank. Interesting furnishings include: slave-made bookcases, "mass production" portraits, much early furniture, chandeliers dating to 1800, French Sevres china of Rose Pompadour, slave-made and Sheffield silver, French bisque figurines, and interesting plantation records. The Orrick Metcalfes own and occupy *The Parsonage.*

On preceding page: Hallway in late afternoon
On opposite page: Front Bedroom

Richmond is a fascinating architectural spectacle. Seemingly, three houses of distinctly different styles have been shoved together to form one forty room mansion. Probably no other house in Natchez has brought about as much disagreement as to its origin and with good reason—logic does not substantiate the claims for its chronological history.

The original section is that of the center. Its date is indefinite as in the case of many an early Natchez house, but some portion possibly was built by John Girault, an Englishman by birth but of French parentage who became an official Spanish translator. His grant from Spain was extensive, and the house called "Richmond Hill" is known to have been built on his tract sometime near 1780. Quite probably *Richmond* was later remodeled by Jean Saint Germain, also a French linguist and interpreter of the Indian language for the Spaniards. These two Frenchmen of the Spanish era would account for this Creole (Spanish-French of Louisiana) type of architecture.

In 1832, *Richmond* was sold by Thomas G. P. Ellis to Levin R. Marshall, a distant relation of the Chief Justice, for $7500, and the following year the new owner added the Greek Revival section.

In regard to the third and remaining section, that of the severe Georgian style portion, there has been disagreement as to its age. Although its date is accepted as 1860 and Marshall's descendants, who still occupy *Richmond,* maintain that he was responsible for its existence, it is difficult to reconcile the facts that a man of such wealth and taste would deliberately create such an incongruity. It is certainly much more logical to assume that had Marshall added the third wing, he would have employed the Greek Revival or a similar style rather than the Georgian which definitely was not in vogue in 1860, that period having ended in 1825.

Regardless of its ancestry, bizarre *Richmond* is a showplace and a favorite of Pilgrimage visitors. Upon entering the house by use of the small Classical Revival portico, with its pure Grecian columns, the visitor finds the main floor hallway opens into bedrooms and double drawing rooms. In the latter, which are separated by double folding doors, there is an impressive ornateness in the black Egyptian marble mantels, the hand-carved woodwork, plaster medallions, and gold cornices over the windows.

The piano of the front drawing room is the most historic of all Natchez. In 1851, the great showman, P. T. Barnum, promoted an American tour for the celebrated coloratura soprano, Jenny Lind, the "Swedish Nightingale." A February concert was to be presented at the Methodist Church, but at the last moment bad weather prevented the movement of Miss Lind's own piano from the steamboat landing up slippery Silver Street. As Levin Marshall volunteered the use of *Richmond's,* the unforgettable concert was able to go on as scheduled.

In the central and brick components of *Richmond* will be found a double dining room, many bedrooms, a play room, and school rooms. The silver service is reputed to be the most ornate in the South, and an amusing exhibit is the Marshalls' collection of early bath tubs, one a hand-pumped shower formerly slave operated.

An interesting historical sidelight was Levin Marshall's financial backing of Sam Houston in Texas. On the large land grant which Marshall received in return, now stands the town of Marshall, Texas.

Richmond

1780-1833-1860

At three it finally stopped growing

Rosalie, high on the river bluff, stands where Natchez got its start.

In 1716, Jean Baptiste le Moyne, Sieur de Bienville, a French explorer, established a fort at this spot and named it "Rosalie" in honor of the wife of the French Minister of Marine, the Count de Pontchartrain. This outpost was not the typical European style of military structure, for it was composed primarily of timber and earthworks and was pentagonal in shape. Today, a replica of one of the fort buildings may be seen just off Canal Street behind *Rosalie,* a location which coincides with one of the original five points of the fort itself; *Rosalie* occupies another of these points.

The story of *Rosalie* is more than just that of the military establishment which once stood here; it is the story of those who built it and those who followed them. Peter B. Little was a very industrious young man who when in his twenties established the first sawmill in the Southwest from a profitable riverboat wreck which he was able to salvage. Later he acquired his wife, Eliza Low, when her parents who were his friends, died from yellow fever and left the girl in his care. Although Eliza was his thirteen year old ward, Peter married her and sent her off to school in Baltimore for several years.

Upon her return, Eliza found that her husband had become an even more prosperous landowner and cotton planter. In about 1820, he had obtained the land near the old fort, and there they built their red brick mansion. The couple employed Peter's brother-in-law, James S. Griffin, from Baltimore, to design and build

their home, and the impressive result exhibited a double-galleried portico complete with classical pediment and supported by four slender Tuscan columns. The name *Rosalie* which the Littles decided upon was an obvious choice.

Some twenty years passed before Peter Little was to build another house, and the reader may find this amusing story in connection with *The Parsonage.*

By 1856 both of the Littles were dead, and *Rosalie* was purchased by their friends, the Andrew L. Wilsons whose descendants lived here until very recent times, even after 1938 when the Daughters of the American Revolution bought the house and restored it.

During the War Between the States, *Rosalie* was used by the Federals as their main headquarters. At this time a rather odd situation existed in that the house had two mistresses when General Walter Q. Gresham occupied the lower floor, and Mrs. Gresham and Mrs. Wilson the upper. The huge gilt-framed mirrors on the walls today once were buried in the garden for safe keeping, and the twenty-four piece set of Belter rosewood furniture was removed, at General Gresham's suggestion, to another location for the same purpose. After the Greshams had left, it was discovered that Mrs. Wilson had long been a member of the Confederate underground, and she was banished to Atlanta for "safe keeping."

Today's pilgrim may view the Gresham bedroom and that of Ulysses S. Grant who visited briefly. A table is also shown at which General Grant and, earlier, Jefferson Davis dined.

On the spot where Natchez began

Rosalie

1820

Stanton Hall, amidst the greenery of its ancient oaks, presents the most imposing facade of all the noble homes of this territory. The double gallery, iron-railed with four massive Corinthian columns and gray and white marble checkerboard floor, was as pretentious as any cotton planter's.

Completed late in 1857 after some half-dozen years of construction by Frederick Stanton, an Irish emigrant who became wealthy as a commission merchant during the great pre-war cotton era, the huge house required such a quantity of furnishings that it was necessary to charter an entire boat to bring them from Europe.

Originally christened "Belfast" after Stanton's town in Ireland, it was said to be a replica of his ancestral home, and when first occupied required the services of seventeen house servants. Frederick Stanton was never to enjoy fully the splendor of his home; he died shortly after its completion.

During the war years that followed, *Stanton Hall* was to receive its share of the punishment too. A cannon ball from a Union gunboat struck and lodged in one Corinthian gallery column, and later Federal troops occupied the house. After those difficult days, the Stanton family was able to retain the mansion until 1894 when it became the Stanton College for Young Ladies. Later, hard times were to see the house sell for less than the cost of the fence around it.

The Pilgrimage Garden Club purchased *Stanton Hall* for its headquarters in 1940 and restored it to its original magnificence.

Among the many impressive antiquities today's visitor may view within its gleaming white walls are enormous gold leaf mirrors at each end of a seventy-two-foot ballroom formed by the combination of the music room and parlor whose ceilings are over twenty-two feet high. Here, in addition to the pair of elaborately carved white Carrara marble mantels with full-sized replicas of fruits and flowers, is an equally elaborate carved arch which was hand crafted in Italy. Architecturally praiseworthy, this feature is afforded no support from the floor.

This is a house of impressive proportions further evidenced by its mahogany entrance door two and one-half inches thick and the sixteen and a half-foot high ceiling of the hallway which runs the length of the house, broken only by another handsomely carved overhead arch. The mahogany stairway which occupies a recessed hall rises to form a rotunda at the third floor after a series of eliptical loops.

On the second floor are six spacious bedrooms luxurious with their period furnishings and available as overnight accommodations for the Natchez pilgrim throughout the year.

The black-bronze chandeliers of *Stanton Hall* are without a doubt the most unusual in the city. Those of the library are decorated with figures of French soldiers complete with weapons and armor, and in the twenty-two by forty-foot banquet hall adjoining, Indian warriors on horseback with bows and arrows ride in bronze circles further depicting early Natchez history.

The craftsmanship and expense lavished upon *Stanton Hall* is clearly revealed in the hand-carved woodwork, the solid silver hardware, and the lacy iron grill work of rose design on the porches which was imported from Italy.

Stanton Hall

1851-1857

Grandeur from Southern cotton

On following pages: Katherine Miller portrait in ballroom.
Chandelier in banquet hall

Twin Oaks, a house that has borne about as many different names
as it has had owners since its erection in 1814, is thought to have
been built by Lewis Evans, first territorial sheriff of Mississippi.
It is a charming white brick of modified Greek design on Homochitto Street shaded by one of the two original oaks that long ago
gave the house its current name. *Twin Oaks* stands on land that
like *Dunleith* was once part of Jeremiah Routh's holdings, an early
British grant. Now occupied by Dr. Homer Whittington and family, it contains such items as an early custom made Steinway grand
piano, and a fourteen piece French rosewood drawing room suite.
The solid silver door hardware, which was probably painted to save
it during occupation times, was discovered years later when a work-
man accidentally touched it with acid.

Additional Ante-Bellum

Auburn, formerly the property of Dr. Stephen Duncan who migrated to Natchez in 1808 from Carlisle, Pennsylvania, was donated in 1911 to the city by his heirs as a memorial. Known as Duncan Park, the grounds are maintained for the recreation of the local citizens, and the house is open to the public without charge.

Levi Weeks, the architect and builder, erected *Auburn* in about 1812 claiming it was the first house in Mississippi Territory on which any of the Orders of Architecture were ever attempted. Quite possibly this was true if the remodeling of *Gloucester* with its Roman Doric-like columns had not been completed by then. Weeks had reason to be proud of his craftsmanship for *Auburn's* front portico is superb with its four great Ionic columns and its carved and paneled doorways.

Stephen Duncan, a physician, banker, sugar and cotton planter, one of America's first millionaires, race horse fancier, owner of some five hundred slaves, and finally a Northern sympathizer at Civil War time, obtained this house upon the death of its owner, his friend, Lyman Harding. His position in life brought him the friendship of such celebrities as Henry Clay,

Edward Everett Hale, and John Howard Payne, and it is recorded that upon one occasion Dr. Duncan was the attending physician for the famous duel between the victorious George Poindexter, a governor of Mississippi and United States Senator, and the rich merchant, Abijah Hunt, who died on the Vidalia sandbar.

Inside *Auburn,* each floor has a pleasant arrangement of six rooms. Downstairs the rooms are equally divided by a great hall and consist of a banquet hall, a drawing room, a library, a "family" dining room, a smoking room, and a smaller drawing room. Upstairs there are six large bedrooms, divided equally by a repeat of the great hall below.

Very worthy of note is *Auburn's* hand-carved woodwork, the vaulted hallways and triple-hung windows, but its most often praised feature is the "geometrical staircase," as Weeks referred to it, which spirals unattached except at each floor level. The antique furnishings, similar to the originals, were donated by women's clubs of Natchez.

Of interest is the great tree at the front, a member of the Live Oak Society of America.

Auburn
1812

Home of an early millionaire

On following page: Auburn's famous stairway

Belmont, east of town on Liberty Road, is a handsome and sturdy edifice built during the Greek Revival period sometime near 1840. Loxley Thistle, its builder, called it "Cleremont," and had it constructed with a massive strength in its thick walls to resist high winds, for a tornado had struck Natchez in 1840. The large cellars of *Belmont* contain underground cisterns in whose cold waters milk was chilled in long, metal buckets made especially for that purpose. In 1854 the house was the scene of the wedding of General William T. Martin and Margaret Conner, later of *Monteigne.* *Belmont* is now owned by Mrs. Louis Fry and daughter, Mrs. Marjory F. Davis.

Belvidere, the diminutive ante-bellum gem located next to *Dunleith,* was moved from the center of a fourteen acre tract, part of which it still occupies. Dating from the 1820's, floor-length windows indicate that it once had a full-length front gallery of Spanish Colonial style. The land formerly belonged to Christopher Miller, secretary of the Spanish governor of Natchez, Gayoso de Lemos, although it is thought the house was built by Robert S. Patterson, later a victim of the 1840 Natchez tornado. Greenebury Kelly and Mrs. Ellen Kelly Goodell of *Belvidere* own much rare glass and china; of particular interest are eighteenth century silhouettes of the first mayor of Natchez, Samuel Brooks, and his wife.

Brandon Hall, located near Selma, eight miles northeast of Natchez, was completed in 1856. Its builder, Gerard Brandon III, was a grandson of the first Gerard Brandon, a North Irish emigrant who, forced to flee during the uprisings, eventually settled in Mississippi on a Spanish grant and established near-by Selma Plantation. Originally planted in indigo, *Brandon Hall* later became a large pecan farm started by a gift from a stranger, a handful of pecans. The galleried house, a modified colonial, has little in common with its Greek Revival period except the Ionic columns. Mr. and Mrs. L. A. White own *Brandon Hall.*

Cherry Grove, built in 1788 by Pierre Surget, was partially destroyed by fire during the 1860's, but re-built upon the same foundation using some of its original timbers which are held together by wooden peg method. Mr. Surget, one of the earliest and wealthiest of Natchez planters, had run away from home in France to become a sailor. Later he purchased his first land from Indians with a cargo of pig iron. *Cherry Grove,* however, was on an initial Spanish grant of twenty-five hundred acres and has always remained in the hands of Surget's descendants. Pierre Surget and his family are buried in the plantation cemetery. Mrs. Grace M. McNeil, owner of *Cherry Grove,* has recently restored and opened this historic place to the public as a guest house. The M. Scott Honnolls are hosts here.

Choctaw, on the corner of Wall and High Streets across from *Cherokee,* was formerly situated with much ground around it including terraced gardens. Records indicate the house was built by Joseph Neibert about 1835, but deeded to Alvarez Fisk about 1840, and has always been known by the local inhabitants as "the old Fisk home" rather than *Choctaw.* Mr. Fisk, a philanthropic merchant, donated properties to found the first free schools here in 1845. Charlestonian in style with massive stone Ionic columned portico, *Choctaw* has recently been restored by the American Legion. Of note is the simulated Indian weapon motif on gallery woodwork.

Cottage Gardens received its name from the extensive plantings which formerly surrounded it, the gardens falling victim to occupying Union cavalry horses. Its builder unknown, the house dates from around 1793. Don Jose Vidal, a high Spanish official now buried in the Natchez Cemetery, once owned the place. Vidal commanded the Vidalia post and buried his wife, Donna, on the high bluffs so he could see her grave from across the river. *Cottage Gardens'* full gallery with pediment is supported by square posts; an unusual and beautiful middle-of-the-hall stairway may be seen here. Mrs. Helen M. R. Foster and her daughter, Mrs. Earl Norman, widow of the late well-known photographer, reside here.

Edgewood is a handsomely situated home whose architectural style
belies its period, the early 1850's. Located in the Pine Ridge section
northeast of Natchez, the house occupies a portion of the 1782 Spanish land grant to John Bisland. It is said that Jane Bisland Lambdin,
wife of its builder, Samuel H. Lambdin, cared little for display and
had *Edgewood* reflect her quiet tastes. James Reid Lambdin, the
famous portrait artist and brother of Samuel, accomplished much
of his finest work here. Of interest are the double Corinthian columns of the front portico. *Edgewood* is now the home of the
Richard A. Campbells.

Glenfield, a quaint brick Gothic cottage, dates in part from about 1812, its early section having hickory pegged beams. The name is actually of comparatively recent origin, Mrs. Verna Lee Field being the owner; previously it was known as "Glencannon" when owned by William Cannon. The grounds, formerly terraced gardens, were the scene of a brisk skirmish during the War, a bullet-scarred door still bearing mute testimony. Other evidence such as medals, buttons, and a soldier's grave have been found near by. Among many unusual items here is a hickory spinning wheel saved from a burning house which had been attacked by Indians, and later brought to Natchez by covered wagon.

Jefferson College, founded in 1802 while Mississippi was still a territory under the American governor, William C. C. Claiborne, is one of America's oldest colleges. Located at Washington, Mississippi, the college first consisted of two small structures. Jefferson Davis attended school here at the age of ten, and once John James Audubon was a faculty member. Near the front gate are the "Aaron Burr Oaks" which shaded the courthouse scene of Burr's preliminary treason trial. Lafayette reviewed cadets here in 1825, and it is said Andrew Jackson and his troops encamped near by in 1813 and again after the Battle of New Orleans in 1815.

King's Tavern, formerly known as the Bledsoe House, was transferred to Richard King in 1789. Its erection date is unknown, but it is considered the oldest structure in Mississippi having been built during the English occupation before the Spanish seizure of 1779. Its timbers, held together with wooden pegs, evidently came from sailing ships, rope holes offering proof. Similar to a fort block house, it stood at one end of the Natchez Trace, a goal of the traveler. The legends of its ghosts are many, but a jeweled dagger which fell from a secret niche and three skeletons unearthed in the cellar are more tangibly romantic. The owner is Mrs. Jeanne Register Modesitt.

Melmont located on North Rankin between B and Oak Streets, has not an architecture of a specific style although the facade suggests a modified Greek Revival. The house, dating from 1854, is of brick with square-pillared double-galleried portico; the land was originally of sufficient elevation to inspire the last syllable of its name. Mary Elizabeth Lattimore lent her initials to form the first syllable when she married *Melmont's* builder, Henry B. Shaw. After being shelled in 1862 by Federal riverboats, the house was later occupied as a Union officers' quarters. Long associated with the Henderson family, *Melmont* is now owned by Mr. and Mrs. Irving Oberlin.

Myrtle Terrace, built sometime near 1830 and located at the corner of High and North Pearl Streets, is a small, colonial type cottage which is often termed "Mississippi Planter." Behind its ornate front iron fence lived one of Natchez's most fabulous characters, Captain Thomas P. Leathers. He purchased *Myrtle Terrace* in 1854 from the N. L. Carpenters, later of *Dunleith*. Captain Leathers became immortalized when as master of the steamboat, *Natchez,* on June 30, 1870, he raced from New Orleans to St. Louis for a $20,000 prize and lost to Captain John Cannon of the *Robert E. Lee*. *Myrtle Terrace* is now the home of Mr. and Mrs. McVey Butler.

Oakland is located on Liberty Road across from *Monteigne,* its name inspired by its oak-lined drive. Dating from 1838, its architecture appears to be a variation of the "Southern Planter" style. For many years it was the residence of the Minor family descended from Stephen Minor, last Natchez governor of the Spaniards. Containing most of its original furnishings, it also has many of those from *Concord,* Minor's residence which no longer exists. Unusual items include: a pier table and mirror from *Concord,* pink, black, and white marble mantels, and a Boston sideboard with carved animals. *Oakland* is the residence of the Alan Ward Granings.

Pleasant Hill, at its present location on Pearl Street near
Orleans, represents an engineering accomplishment seldom if ever
equaled during its time. Built sometime around 1803, it formerly
occupied a "pleasant hill" one block north, but about 1850 was
moved by Thomas Henderson, a feat which involved lowering the
building to street level and then rolling it; the process took almost
two years. The house is much more spacious than it appears, its tiny
portico increasing the deception. Unusual furnishings include: carved
rosewood, a French piano, a black marble-topped fishtail table, and
Windsor chairs. Residing here is Mrs. Lathrop Postlethwaite, a
name long associated with *Pleasant Hill.*

Propinquity, near Washington, northeast of Natchez, stands in a wooded section not far from a stretch of the original Natchez Trace. It is believed to have been there when General Leonard Covington purchased the property from Beverly R. Grayson in 1811. Covington named his home "Propinquity" as its lands adjoined Fort Dearborn where he commanded the Light Dragoons. Two years later Covington lost his life fighting at the Battle of Chrysler's Farm on the St. Lawrence River in Canada. Cities in Kentucky and Louisiana are named for him. Interesting items here include hand-painted window shades and a carved wooden mantel with removable urns. More recently *Propinquity* was the home of Mrs. M. E. Fauntleroy, a descendant of the celebrated Jane Long, "Mother of Texas."

Ravenna, near the end of South Union Street, is a large, two-story Colonial type, its handsome double-galleried front showing Doric columns below and Ionic above. William Harris built *Ravenna* about 1836, and shortly afterwards saw it unroofed in the Natchez tornado of May, 1840. During the War, the Federals ousted the Oren Metcalfes claiming Mrs. Zuleika Metcalfe was smuggling supplies through Union lines using the near-by bayou from which ravine came the house's name. *Ravenna's* hallway is one of Natchez's most handsome. Of particular note are the gardens with their azaleas, dogwood, and wisteria. Mr. and Mrs. Albert Dickens Williams now own *Ravenna.*

Routhland, located on Winchester Road, with its wide gallery
and slender colonettes is similar to many another early planter type,
and like many another early home, its actual erection date is unknown. Situated on a Spanish grant of 1792, *Routhland* may have
been built shortly thereafter, as a dwelling was required by law.
John Routh, son of the wealthy Job, was deeded the property in
1824 but used it only as a summer home. Wartime governor and
hero, General Charles Clark, bought *Routhland* in 1871. Today,
occupied by Mrs. Laurie Ratcliffe and family, it is somewhat modern-
ized but elegantly furnished with antiques. With its sweeping lawn
and moss draped oaks, it is a picturesque representative of the
"old South."

Springfield, about fifteen miles northeast of Natchez, is important historically as the marriage place of Andrew Jackson and Rachel Donelson Robards. Thomas Green, Sr., father of the builder, a personal friend of Jackson and a distant relation of Rachel, was the magistrate who officiated at the ceremony. About 1791, Thomas Marston Green built *Springfield* which was the largest brick mansion in this vicinity for many years. Two and one-half stories it still stands with sloping roof shading double galleries supported by six tall white Roman Doric columns. Indicative of its age are the two-foot thick walls, low narrow windows, massive doors, and low ceilings. *Springfield* is owned by Mrs. James H. Williams, Sr., James H. Williams, Jr., and William P. Williams.

The Towers dates back to about 1818, the back section being known in its early days as "Gardenia Cottage" when Charles Dicks lived there. The famed architect, Samuel Sloan, added the towered front in 1841 for William Chamberlain, but the top sections forming the towers burned in 1927. During the Civil War, Union soldiers occupied the house, one of whom was the "unpopular" Colonel Hayes, Chief Engineer. Out of spite, Hayes ordered *Clifton,* the near-by showplace of Frank Surget II, destroyed, for its owner had overlooked sending the officer a party invitation. *The Towers* is the residence of Mrs. Maude E. Varnado.

Weymouth Hall, north of town on Cemetery Road, is a three-storied, double-galleried house whose roof-top captain's walk overlooks the river, a vantage point that caused its commandeering by Union forces. John Weymouth completed this curiously planned structure in 1852 after his first house near by was destroyed by the tornado of 1840. Although definitely Spanish in flavor, its architecture is an odd yet very pleasant blend of several types. A unique feature of the house is a living room mantel made of black marble inlaid with colored roses of mother of pearl. The Zurhellen and Morton families reside here.

The Wigwam, situated near the corner of Oak Street and Myrtle Avenue across from *The Towers,* is another of the very old buildings of Natchez. No definite date is known for its construction, but it certainly was standing in 1819. Mrs. Robert O. Lowry, owner of *The Wigwam,* suggests that it might be as old as any house in town; however, its architectural style does not seem to be Spanish with the broad hallway dividing its rooms, and its ironwork was admittedly a later addition. Its name evolved from three ancient near-by Indian mounds. The hallway's oval plaster work medallion is still exquisite, and the library with its hand-decorated walls depicting the four seasons is unduplicated elsewhere.

And Now They Belong to the Ages . . .

During the last fifty years more than forty of the ante-bellum houses in the Natchez district have been lost to fire, windstorm, or decay. Some of these were celebrated, some were nameless, but each was a romantic link with the past now gone forever except in book or memory. Their names fall pleasantly upon the ear. *Magnolia Vale, Glenwood, Clermont, Concord, Inglewood, Somerset, Windy Hill,* these and many more have passed from view, each like a theatre in itself with its players, their entrances, their exits. Many are the tales told about them, and more often than not these true stories are stranger than any fiction.

Homewood was perhaps the most palatial of all those now gone. Designed for William Balfour and his wife, the former Catherine Hunt from *Woodlawn,* construction began in 1855 and continued for some five years. One million bricks were burned on the grounds for use in its two and a half-foot thick walls. Thirty-foot Grecian Ionic metal columns supporting a massive pediment, a small ironwork balcony similar to *D'Evereux's,* and double-decked ironwork galleries on each side of the house, all imported from Spain, gave the exterior a definite Gulf Coast touch. Four halls downstairs leading to four entrances formed a

114

Greek cross. The twelve rooms of the house, six down and six up, were huge. Their refinements, mantles of white marble, one of pink marble with gray veins, one of pink marble with deep rose tracings, solid silver door knobs, hinges and locks, were impressive.

When Mr. and Mrs. Kingsley Swan of New York acquired *Homewood* in the 1930's, their furnishings of Chippendale, Sheraton, and Louis XVI were strictly in keeping with its grandeur. Then one night, January 2, 1940, it was gone. The fire fighters fought valiantly, but Mrs. Swan and a large segment of the Natchez citizenry watched majestic *Homewood's* flaming death.

Concord, a truly historic structure and one of the very earliest mansions of Natchez having been erected in 1794, joined the departed in 1901, also a victim of fire. Its builder, the Spanish governor, Don Manuel Gayoso de Lemos, perhaps created a style of his own. At the time of its demise anyway, *Concord* was a blend unparalleled. Two and one-half stories with full length galleries at the second level gave it a flavor of the Spanish West Indies. The Classic Revival front, however, with its pediment and Tuscan-like columns rising two floors tall gives one the impression that it must have been an afterthought of the 1830's. In

all fairness we should assume that and give Don Manuel the benefit of the doubt. One feature of *Concord* worth mentioning was the carriage drive under the central portion of the house. Beneath the portico, the entrance, flanked on each side by two curving flights of iron-railed marble steps, became a tunnel formed by the walls of the storerooms and stables of the lower floor.

Concord was an odd house, and it is fitting that an odd story accompanies its end. Mrs. George M. D. Kelly, present owner of *Melrose,* had arrived in Natchez with her husband shortly after they had inherited *Concord.* The very first time she laid eyes on the house, it was afire.

For years, the ruins of *Concord* stood at Gayoso and LaSalle Streets. Little by little they disappeared as people borrowed from them until only the curving front steps and a column or two were standing. Finally, one flight of steps remained, then in 1958 these, too, disappeared.

And so they go—a careless match here, a faulty wire there, or an unpreventable lightning bolt. All that those of us who love them can do is to cherish them, record them, enjoy them while they are still here, and hope fervently that they will be spared for future generations.

Horses lived on the lower floor

Concord

1794

Homewood

1860

Don Esteban Minor House. This structure, dating back to the eighteenth century, was located at 44 St. Catherine Street. At one time it had been the home of the last acting governor for Spain prior to his purchase in 1799 of *Concord,* the mansion of former Governor Manuel Gayoso de Lemos. Don Esteban Minor's bride, Katherine Lintot, became one of the fabulous characters of Natchez, and acquired the nickname, "The Yellow Duchess," because of her affinity for that color. Her house furnishings, her carriage, her servants and, they say, even her pantaloons were golden yellow. Long in a condition of deterioration, this house was razed during 1958.

Glenwood was once a proud ante-bellum residence dating from the
1830's. It gained national prominence in 1932 during the Jennie
Merrill murder case when its occupants, Richard Dana and Octavia
Dockery, two cultured and talented people in their youth, were
accused but never tried. Miss Merrill had been found murdered on
the grounds of her neighboring *Glenburnie,* and the two eccentrics
of *Glenwood* (both now deceased) were suspected because of a
previous quarrel involving their trespassing goats. Dana's roving
animals had free run of *Glenwood* and caused its nickname, "Goat
Castle." The site of this house, now located appropriately on Dana
Road, is within a new residential district.

Windy Hill Manor, nine miles east of Natchez out Liberty Road was an early plantation dating to 1797 that was first known as "Halfway Hill" when Colonel Benijah Osmun built it. Here Aaron Burr, while awaiting trial, was a guest of honor and courted the neighborhood beauty, Madeline Price, who, although charmed by the scoundrel, refused to flee with him. Traces of the gardens and walks where they met still remain. From about 1820 the house belonged to the Brandon and Stanton families, descendants of whom occupied it until recently. Miss Elizabeth Brandon Stanton was a historian of note and author of *Fata Morgana,* a novel that dealt with the intrigue of Aaron Burr. The house was demolished in 1956.

Final days of a grand old house

Windsor, tradition says, was named by the local citizens who heard the wind moaning through its columns. Situated some thirty miles northeast of Natchez, it boasted of five stories and an observatory on the roof which Mark Twain often used as a landmark from the river. The great columns were of brick plastered with fluted stucco to resemble stone and crowned with huge Corinthian capitals of New Orleans cast iron. Smith C. Daniell completed the house in 1861, but death prevented his witnessing its occupation as a Union army hospital during Grant's Vicksburg campaign of 1863. It was later destroyed by a fire of unknown origin in 1890. The ruins figured prominently in the motion picture, "Raintree County."

On following page: Windsor's columns stab dramatically at the sky

Natchez Under-the-Hill

Once Silver Street meant violence and sin

BIBLIOGRAPHY

A Guide to Early American Homes—South. Dorothy and Richard Pratt. New York, 1956.

A Treasury of Early American Homes. Richard Pratt. New York, 1949.

A Treasury of Mississippi River Folklore. B. A. Botkin. New York, 1955.

A Treasury of Southern Folklore. B. A. Botkin. New York, 1949.

American Guide, The. Henry G. Alsberg. New York, 1949.

American Heritage. Bruce Catton, Editor. Vol. VIII, No. 6. New York, 1957.

Audubon. Constance Rourke. New York, 1936.

Gentlemen, Swords and Pistols. Harnett T. Kane. New York, 1951.

Homes of America, The. Ernest Pickering. New York, 1951.

Lower Mississippi. Hodding Carter. New York, 1942.

Natchez A Treasure of Ante-Bellum Homes. J. Wesley Cooper, Natchez, Miss., 1957.

Natchez, Mississippi Views. Tom L. Ketchings. Natchez, Miss.

Natchez on the Mississippi. Harnett T. Kane. New York, 1947.

Natchez Symbol of the Old South. Nola Nance Oliver. New York, 1940.

Natchez Under-the-Hill. Edith Wyatt Moore. Natchez, Miss., 1958.

Plantation Parade. Harnett T. Kane. New York, 1945.

White Pillars. J. Frazer Smith. New York, 1941.

In addition to many standard works of reference, including some encyclopedias now long out of print, several editions of the newspapers, *The Natchez Times* and *The Natchez Democrat,* were consulted.

Acknowledgments

Grateful acknowledgment is extended to the many helpful citizens of Natchez and its immediate vicinity for their courteous cooperation and cordial assistance in the preparation of this book. In addition to the members of the Natchez Garden Club and the Pilgrimage Garden Club, I wish especially to acknowledge the efforts and courtesies of the following: Mrs. Hubert Barnum; Mrs. George M. D. Kelly; Mrs. R. Hicks Parker; Mrs. Ellen Kelly Goodell; Mrs. Edith Wyatt Moore, prominent author, lecturer, and Historian of the Natchez Garden Club; and Mrs. J. Balfour Miller, the guiding light of each and every Natchez Pilgrimage.

R. G. P.

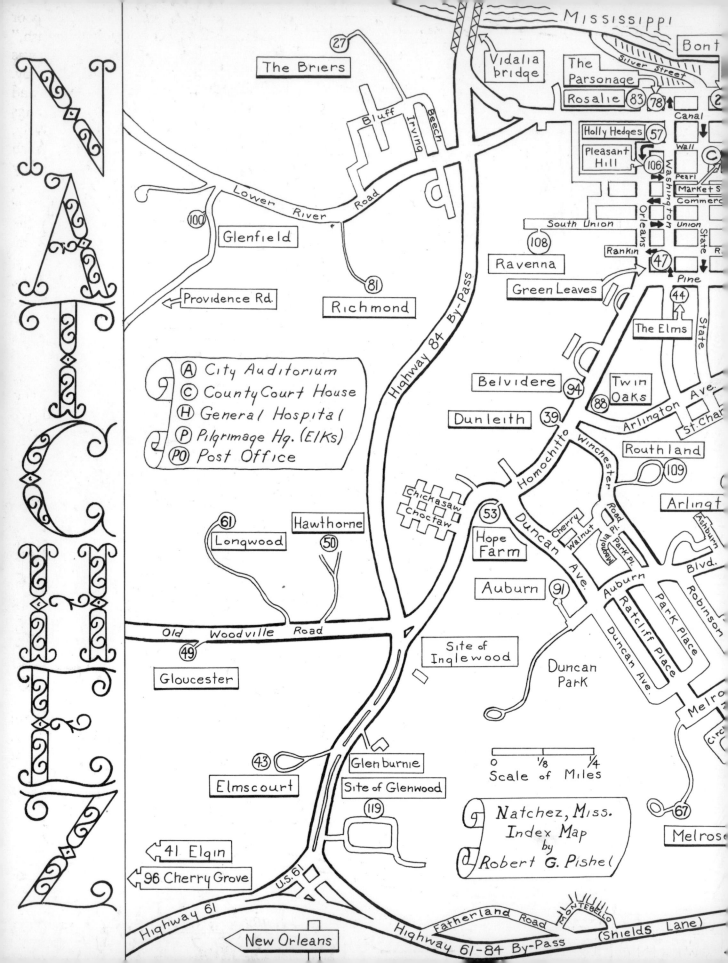